ÄGAR

Hagar [illegible]ough

DIK BROWNE

ATTICA
PUBLICATIONS

Introducing . . .

HÄGAR THE HORRIBLE a hard-working Barbarian businessman. He's in sacking and looting.

His wife, HELGA. She finds civilising Hägar a 24-hour-a-day job!

This is HAMLET, their son, a real problem child! He insists on wearing his hair short, bathing, reading and otherwise behaving in a very unbarbarian manner.

HONI, their daughter, is sixteen years old, and still not married!

But that's not the end of Hägars troubles . . . there's also LUCKY EDDIE who must be the most hopeless assistant in history!

First published by ATTICA Publications 1986.

ATTICA Publications is an imprint of ATTICA Ltd., DLM House, Edinburgh Way, Harlow, Essex, CM20 2HL, England.

ISBN 1 85176 027 X

Printed and bound in Great Britain by Cox & Wyman Ltd, Reading

ONLY ONE PIECE LEFT— WANT TO FLIP ME FOR IT?
OKAY
FLIP!
SIGH
NOW THAT WAS POORLY WORDED
DIK BROWNE

I WISH HAMLET WAS MORE LIKE OTHER BOYS
WHY? THEY'RE JUST RUFFIANS!

I KNOW, BUT AT LEAST THEY'RE LEARNING A TRADE!
DIK BROWNE

IS THIS SHIELD ANY GOOD?
SIR! WE STAND BEHIND OUR PRODUCTS!
DIK BROWNE

FIGURATIVELY SPEAKING, OF COURSE!

IT'S LATE—I HOPE WE'RE NOT KEEPING YOU FOLKS UP
CERTAINLY NOT! CAN I GET YOU SOMETHING ELSE?

HOW ABOUT BREAKFAST?
DIK BROWNE

I HATE COCKTAIL PARTIES!
STOP GRUMBLING... I TOLD YOU, AS SOON AS YOU GET BORED, SIGNAL ME AND WE'LL GO HOME

WILL YOU WAIT TILL I GET MY COAT OFF ?!!

I TOLD YOU TO WASH MY SAIL IN COLD WATER!
SO WHAT?

YOU SHRINK EVERYTHING!
DIK BROWNE

NICE TIME TO BE COMING HOME!

YOU TOO!!
DIK BROWNE

"THE SEA OF NO-RETURN"! HOW WILL WE FIND OUR WAY BACK?
I THOUGHT OF THAT

LUCKY EDDIE IS LEAVING A TRAIL OF BREAD CRUMBS
DIK BROWNE

DIK BROWNE

TO BE A TRUE VIKING — NEVER EXPLAIN! NEVER APOLOGIZE!
I DON'T UNDERSTAND

I'M SORRY... I PROBABLY DIDN'T EXPLAIN THAT PROPERLY... IT MEANS...
DIK BROWNE

To Helga ~ A GREAT WIFE, WONDERFUL HOMEMAKER, LOVING MOTHER ...
DIK BROWNE

AND WORTHY OPPONENT
THANK YOU

SINCE WHEN HAS DADDY BEEN *HAPPY* TO TAKE OUT THE GARBAGE?

SINCE WE HAD THAT ARGUMENT WITH OUR NEXT-DOOR NEIGHBOUR
DIK BROWNE

WHAT KIND OF DOG IS THAT ?
IT'S A 'SHADE HOUND'
ARE THEY HARD TO RAISE ?
NO, BUT THEY NEED A SPECIAL TYPE OF OWNER
BROWNE

KIDS ARE A LOT SMARTER THAN THEY USED TO BE
OH, YEAH?

THEN WHERE DO ALL THE DUMB GROWN-UPS COME FROM?
DIK BROWNE

WELCOME TO FLOODVILLE... FAMOUS FOR ITS TERRIBLE TIDES!
WOW! WHEN IS LOW TIDE?
DIK BROWNE

THIS IS LOW TIDE

DON'T YOU DARE LIE TO ME OR YOUR **HORNS WILL FALL OFF!**

NOW TELL ME FROM THE BEGINNING WHAT HAPPENED!

DIK BROWNE
AND DON'T TWIST THE TRUTH!!

HERE THEY COME—JUMP!

BOY! THAT WAS CLOSE!
DIK BROWNE

NOW THAT'S A CHERRY FLIP!
DIK BROWNE

I'VE HAD A ROUGH DAY!
TELL ME LATER. SUPPER IS READY

NOW SIT DOWN AND EAT BEFORE IT GETS COLD
DIK BROWNE 7-12

YES! YES! I'LL GIVE YOU DESSERT!
A BOWL OF SUGAR?
NO TOPPING?
DIK BROWNE

I TOOK THREE ARROWS IN BATTLE TODAY...OBVIOUSLY I CAN TAKE IT... I JUST HAVE ONE REQUEST...
DIK BROWNE

DON'T PUT THE STINGY STUFF ON ME!!

WHILE I'M GONE I WANT YOU TO BE MY EYES AND EARS!
YES, SIR
DIK BROWNE
BUT NOT MY STOMACH!

MY FAMILY WILL SIT IN THE MIDDLE—YOUR FAMILY ON BOTH ENDS
WILL THAT WORK?

YES... IF IT DOESN'T RAIN
DIK BROWNE

ON GUARD! YOU MAY BE BIG BUT I DON'T CARE!
?
I'LL MAKE YOU KNEEL TO ME!
I AM KNEELING!
DIK BROWNE

DOPE! DON'T YOU HAVE ANY MANNERS?!

I TOLD YOU — SERVE FROM THE RIGHT, TAKE AWAY FROM THE LEFT

I'LL SHOW YOU THE GAME THE SCOTS CALL GOLF
OH, GOOD
YOU HIT THIS STONE WITH THIS CLUB
DIK BROWNE
NOW, REMEMBER... KEEP YOUR HEAD DOWN

HEY!
REMEMBER THE FIRST RULE OF A GOOD VIKING!

"DON'T MAKE WAVES!"
DIK BROWNE

AMAZING!!
DIK BROWNE

WHAT DOES IT SAY?
IT SAYS: "THIS ICE IS STRONG ENOUGH TO HOLD 3 NORMAL MEN"

DIK BROWNE

I THOUGHT YOU WERE GOING TO INVADE EUROPE ?!
I AM...

YOU SAY IT BUT YOU DON'T DO IT!!
OKAY! I'M GOING!

ANYTHING TO KEEP PEACE!

MAKE SNERT STOP THAT!!
AW, ALL DOGS BURY BONES...
DIK BROWNE

NOT IN MY KITCHEN!

IT'S CALLED "THE WINE OF FORGETFULNESS"
GOOD, VERY GOOD
HEY, YOU FORGOT TO PAY!
FOR WHAT?
GEE! I HOPE THIS BRAND DOESN'T CATCH ON!
DIK BROWNE

HOW'S HAGAR'S DIET ?
OKAY... HIS PROBLEM WAS ALWAYS SNACKING BETWEEN MEALS...
DIK BROWNE

BUT I THINK WE'VE SOLVED THAT

I'M HERE TO COLLECT THE "HEAD TAX"
MORE NON-SENSE!

WHY IS IT CALLED THE "HEAD TAX" ANYWAY?

GUESS
DIK BROWNE

SORRY, SNERT, I CAN'T PLAY WITH YOU NOW
DIK BROWNE

AND PUT THOSE CARDS BACK

AH! THE BARGAIN HUNTERS!
THE LADIES DO LOVE TO GET A BARGAIN!
YOU'D NEVER KNOW IT BY THE HUSBANDS WE GET!
DIK BROWNE

YOU'RE FAT AND FLABBY, HAGAR! FOR A MAN OF YOUR AGE, I'M AMAZED AT THE SHAPE YOU'RE IN!
DIK BROWNE

WHAT DID THE DOCTOR SAY?
FOR A MAN OF MY AGE, HE WAS AMAZED AT THE SHAPE I'M IN!

ARE WE LIVING IN THE MIDDLE AGES OR THE DARK AGES?
DARK AGES
DIK BROWNE

DAD, WHAT IS LIFE?
LIFE IS FIGHTING, RAIDING, DRINKING BEER, PARTYING AND PLAYING GAMES

THERE HAS TO BE MORE THAN THAT!
THERE IS, BUT I JUST COVERED THE IMPORTANT PARTS
DIK BROWNE

THAT LIVER AND LEEK SOUP IS THE PERFECT FOOD! IT HAS EVERYTHING YOUR BODY NEEDS!
IT'S PERFECT!
AND IT ISN'T HABIT FORMING

I'M FED UP WITH YOU, LUTE! YOU'RE LIKE ALL MUSICIANS—YOU'RE REALLY JUST IN LOVE WITH YOUR MUSIC!
NOT SO, HONI...

AND STOP CALLING OUR ROMANCE A 'GIG'!
DIK BROWNE

KVACK'S BIRTHDAY IS COMING... WHAT CAN I GET FOR A DUCK THAT HAS EVERYTHING?
DIK BROWNE
ORANGE SAUCE
AND YOU WONDER WHY SHE DOESN'T LOVE YOU!

WOMEN ARE A MYSTERY

DIK BROWNE
I LOVE A GOOD MYSTERY

YOUR SMORGASBORD LOOKS DELICIOUS, HELGA!
BUT AFTER MONTHS AT SEA I DON'T KNOW WHAT TO TAKE FIRST!
HOW ABOUT A BATH?
DIK BROWNE

RAGNAR!
HAGAR?!

HOW DID YOU RECOGNIZE ME AFTER ALL THESE YEARS?
ARE YOU KIDDING? I NEVER FORGET A FACE!
DIK BROWNE

IF YOU HADN'T MET ME, WHERE WOULD YOU BE TODAY ?
I HEARD WHAT YOU'RE THINKING!!!
DIK BROWNE

I NEED SOME COPIES OF THIS, PLEASE
THERE WILL BE A SLIGHT DELAY
DIK BROWNE

OUR COPIER HAS BROKEN DOWN
SNIFF SNIFF

WHEN YOU ENTERTAIN MY CREW, STAY AWAY FROM POLITICS... STAY AWAY FROM RELIGION...
STAY AWAY FROM ETHNIC JOKES...STAY AWAY FROM SEXY STUFF...
COME TO THINK OF IT... JUST STAY AWAY
DIK BROWNE

WANT ANYTHING CLEANED?
YES

CAN YOU HAVE HIM BACK BY FRIDAY?
DIK BROWNE

GET UP!
BUT IT'S STILL DARK!
OPEN YOUR EYES, STUPID!!!
DIK BROWNE
OH...

WHAT IS "SHEDDING," MAMA?
THAT'S NATURE'S WAY OF LETTING DUMB ANIMALS GET RID OF THEIR HEAVY WINTER COAT IN THE SPRING
DIK BROWNE

HI, FOLKS— GETTING WARM, ISN'T IT?

DON'T YOU EVER WASH YOUR EARS?
DIK BROWNE
THERE... THAT'S BETTER
WHAT ARE YOU SHOUTING ABOUT?!

HURRY UP! THE WATER'S GETTING COLD AGAIN!
I'M COMING!

THAT'S BETTER
DIK BROWNE

HMMMM...
OH, OH...
TSK, TSK...
DOES LUCKY EDDIE TALK TO PLANTS?
NAW

MMMM...
MY, MY...
OH, DEAR...
HE'S JUST A GOOD LISTENER...
DIK BROWNE

IT WAS THE COLDEST WINTER IN 30 YEARS, BUT AT LEAST WE DIDN'T FREEZE TO DEATH!
THAT'S RIGHT!

I KINDA MISS THE FURNITURE THOUGH...
DIK BROWNE

IT SAYS "WELCOME TO THE GYPSY FOREST"
"FOREST"?

WELL, YOU KNOW HOW GYPSIES EXAGGERATE
DIK BROWNE

THERE IS NO ACCOUNTING FOR THE KIND OF MEN THAT WOMEN FALL IN LOVE WITH
REALLY ?
DIK BROWNE
REALLY !

SORRY, DEAR, BUT I HAVE TO GO VISIT A SICK FRIEND
WHO'S THAT?
A BARTENDER I KNOW WITH SORE FEET
DIK BROWNE

PUH-TOOIE!!
DIK BROWNE

WHAT WAS THAT DUCK STUFFED WITH?!
SAWDUST

YOU CALL YOURSELF A COOK?!
I'M REALLY A TAXIDERMIST

WHILE I'M AWAY, SON, YOU'LL HAVE TO BE THE MAN OF THE HOUSE!
WHAT DOES THAT MEAN, DAD?

YOU HAVE TO EAT TOO MUCH, SLEEP TOO MUCH AND TAKE OUT GARBAGE OCCASIONALLY...
DIK BROWNE

WHAT'S HAPPENING TO THE WORLD? FIRST WE RUN OUT OF GOLD— THEN OIL...
DIK BROWNE

NOW, A WATER SHORTAGE!!

HAGAR WAS A FAMOUS "GIRL WATCHER" WHEN HE WAS YOUNG

OF COURSE HE'S CHANGED A LOT...
DIK BROWNE

I DON'T CARE WHERE YOU GO OR WHAT YOU DO — JUST TELL ME WHEN YOU'LL BE HOME SO I DON'T WAIT DINNER!
OKAY

WELL? WHEN WILL YOU BE BACK?!

DIK BROWNE
LATER

TOUGH WINTER!
AND IT LOOKS LIKE IT'S GOING TO BE A TOUGH SPRING

?
LOOK! A WOOLY BUTTERFLY!
DIK BROWNE

LONDON LADIES HAVE LOVELY SKINS
SKINS?!

NO! NO! I SAID SHINS!
SHINS?!

I SHOULD HAVE STAYED WITH "SKINS"...
DIK BROWNE

HELGA, I HATE TO COMPLAIN—BUT COULD YOU PACK SOMETHING ELSE FOR MY LUNCH FOR A CHANGE?

DIK BROWNE
BUT I THOUGHT YOU LIKED SPAGHETTI

I NEED SOME MONEY
GEE... I DON'T KNOW...

OH
PLINK!
PLINK!
PING!

SHE COULD HAVE BEEN THE GREATEST SACKER AND LOOTER OF THEM ALL ...
DIK BROWNE

NEVER PUT A WOMAN ON A PEDESTAL, LUCKY EDDIE
WHY NOT?

YOU'LL GET A HERNIA
DIK BROWNE

AH! I'M A NEW WOMAN!
DIK BROWNE

BUT DADDY DOESN'T LIKE THAT!
NONSENSE. WHEN I GET THROUGH FANCYING IT UP, HE WON'T KNOW WHAT HE'S GETTING!
DIK BROWNE

LIVER AGAIN?

OUR CLAMS ARE EXCELLENT.
I'LL TRY A DOZEN
MAY I SUGGEST SIX TO START...
THEY'RE RATHER LARGE
DIK BROWNE

BROTHER HAGAR, DON'T YOU BELIEVE IN AN ALL-POWERFUL FORCE THAT GOVERNS OUR LIVES AND WATCHES OUR EVERY MOVE ?

DIK BROWNE
YOU MEAN BESIDES WOMEN ?

HOLD IT! HOLD IT!!

BOY! THAT WAS CLOSE!
WET PAINT
DIK BROWNE

WHY CAN'T I GO WITH YOU TO INVADE ENGLAND, DADDY?
BECAUSE—NICE GIRLS DON'T DO THAT SORT OF THING!

OH, DADDY! THIS IS A.D. CMLXXX NOT CMLXXX B.C.!
DIK BROWNE

MY GOSH! WHAT HAPPENED TO YOU?
AMNESIA
DIK BROWNE

I FORGOT MY WIFE'S BIRTHDAY

...AND THAT FISH WAS THAT BIG! NOW TOP THAT!

WOULD YOU BELIEVE...
DIK BROWNE

YOUR HARD-BOILED EGGS ARE READY
I WANTED THEM SCRAMBLED
BAM!
DIK BROWNE
OKAY, THEY'RE SCRAMBLED

CONCENTRATO EL VOLLYO EN NUMERO UNO!!
WHAT DID HE SAY ?

"TRY TO GET THE FAT GUY FIRST"
DIK BROWNE

I'M A GOBLIN
I DON'T BELIEVE IN GOBLINS!
I DON'T BELIEVE IN FAT GUYS WITH HORNS!
FAIR ENOUGH! HEY! GIVE MY FRIEND A DRINK!
DIK BROWNE

SURPRISE, HELGA! WHILE YOU WERE OUT I MADE DINNER!
OH, GOOD! WHAT ARE WE HAVING?
TOMATO SOUP, CREAMED CORN, APPLESAUCE, ROAST BEEF AND CHOCOLATE PUDDING
DIK BROWNE

NO MATTER WHAT SHE SAYS — JUST AGREE WITH HER!
LOOK AT THE TIME!! DO YOU THINK I'M A FOOL?!!
ANY OTHER ADVICE?

YOU SHOULD MEASURE YOUR DRINKS—USE A SHOT GLASS

THIS IS MY SHOT GLASS
DIK BROWNE

IS IT TRUE THAT "NICE GUYS FINISH LAST"?
NAW!

NOT ALWAYS!
DIK BROWNE

WHAT'S IN THE POKE ?
I BOUGHT A PIG
OINK!
DIK BROWNE

I DON'T THINK IT'S A GOOD IDEA TO BUY A PIG IN A POKE
I'M NOT TOO CRAZY ABOUT IT EITHER!
OINK
OINK

TELL ME, WISE ONE... WHY DO YOU LIVE ON A MOUNTAIN, DRESS IN RAGS AND SLEEP IN A CAVE?
DIK BROWNE
IT'S A TAX DODGE
HEY! YOU ARE A WISE MAN!

HOW WAS YOUR DAY?
THAT BAD, EH?
DIK BROWNE

AND WHAT'LL YOU HAVE?

IF IT'S NOT TOO MUCH TROUBLE, I'D LIKE AN EXTRA DRY MARTINI–VERMOUTH ON THE SIDE AND HOLD THE OLIVE.

DIK BROWNE
CHECK

WHAT IS THE MEANING OF LIFE? WHY AM I HERE?
DIK BROWNE
BECAUSE IF YOU WERE HOME YOU'D HAVE TO HELP WITH THE DISHES, RIGHT?

DO YOU THINK YOU COULD UNTIE THE BOAT ?
OF COURSE! WHAT AM I ? —STUPID ?!
SORRY... WRONG ROPE...
DIK BROWNE

MAMA, DID YOU JUST MAKE A BATCH OF FUDGE ?
YES...

AND DID YOU TELL DADDY HE COULD LICK THE POT ?
YES...
DIK BROWNE

THAT EXPLAINS THAT.

STOP COMPLAINING! I TREAT YOU LIKE A KING! YOU HEAR ME ?!

A KING!
YEAH... YEAH...

IVAN THE TERRIBLE!
DIK BROWNE

SHOULDN'T HAGAR HAVE THAT OUT ?
OH, YOU KNOW MEN—AFRAID TO GO TO THE DOCTOR

HE'D RATHER WALK AROUND LOOKING LIKE A CHICKEN !
DIK BROWNE

I SWEAR — SOME DOGS ARE JUST LIKE HUMANS!
DIK BROWNE

THEY EVEN SEEM TO KNOW WHEN YOU ARE WORRIED

HAGAR, DO YOU BELIEVE IN MYTHICAL BEASTS AND MONSTERS?
NAW!
DIK BROWNE

OH, THANK GOODNESS!

HAMLET, SEE IF YOUR FATHER IS READY FOR DINNER...
YES, MAMA
DIK BROWNE

HE'S READY

HAGAR, I'D LIKE YOU TO MEET "ERIC THE BALD"

DIK BROWNE
BOLD! BOLD! "ERIC THE BOLD"!

WHAT ARE YOU DOING WITH THAT SHOVEL, MAMA?
SAVING TIME!
DIK BROWNE

OPEN WIDE!

OH, DADDY! REMEMBER, YOU WERE YOUNG ONCE YOURSELF!

YOU'RE RIGHT!—I REMEMBERED!
DIK BROWNE

EVER NOTICE HOW DOGS SEEM TO SENSE FEAR IN A PERSON?

YES
DIK BROWNE

MY STOMACH DON'T FEEL GOOD!
WHAT DID YOU EAT?
NOT MUCH... A COUPLE OF CHICKENS, A LEG OF MUTTON, SOME KIDNEY PIES, HOG SOUP... SOME OLIVES...
DIK BROWNE
WELL, YOU KNOW OLIVES DON'T AGREE WITH YOU!

OKAY, SON—SHOOT!
AW, I MISSED AGAIN!

OKAY, LET'S TRY A BIGGER TARGET
DIK BROWNE

MAMA, HOW WILL I KNOW "MR. RIGHT"?
DON'T WORRY, HONI— YOU'LL KNOW—STARS WILL APPEAR...TIME WILL STOP...
DIK BROWNE
BUT HOW WILL I KNOW HE'S REALLY "MR. RIGHT" ?
DON'T WORRY— YOUR MOTHER WILL TELL YOU

SNERT IS A LONG-TAILED COCKER-BOXER SCHNAUZER
YOU MEAN A MUTT
DIK BROWNE

SNERT'S VERY SENSITIVE ABOUT HIS PARENTAGE

WHAT SHAPE AM I IN, DOCTOR ZOOK?
DIK BROWNE
I HATE SARCASTIC DOCTORS.

DON'T WORRY, HAMLET, I USED TO BE LITTLE LIKE YOU...

THEN ONE DAY- ≥POOF≤ I SHOT UP!

...AND THEN ≥POOF≤ HE SHOT OUT!
DIK BROWNE

A LEG CAST ALWAYS FEELS UNCOMFORTABLE AT FIRST- BUT YOU'LL GET USED TO IT

NOW, WHAT DID I DO WITH MY HAMMER ?
DIK BROWNE

I'D LIKE TO DO SOMETHING THAT WOULD BE REMEMBERED AND TALKED ABOUT FOREVER!

FORGET YOUR WIFE'S BIRTHDAY
DIK BROWNE

THE ENEMY IS AT THE GATES!
HURRY WITH THE BOILING OIL!!

IN A MINUTE!
YOU WANT FRIED CHICKEN, DON'T YOU?
DIK BROWNE

WE FRIENDS!
THEY DON'T UNDERSTAND

WHAT WILL WE DO?
TRY SIGN LANGUAGE

DIK BROWNE
WE FRIENDS!

I THINK I'M GOING TO WEAR THIS DRESS "OFF THE SHOULDER"
I WOULDN'T...
DIK BROWNE
KLUNK!
NOT WITH HEAVY ARMOR

WHAT'S THE SOUP TODAY?
TOMATO SOUP
BLAH! I HATE TOMATOES!
NO PROBLEM
ONE BOWL OF SOUP — HOLD THE TOMATOES!
DIK BROWNE

NO, HELGA! I AM NOT COMING DOWN FOR A BATH!
DIK BROWNE
AND THERE'S NOTHING YOU CAN DO ABOUT IT!
CHOP CHOP CHOP

STAY CLEAR OF HELGA TODAY—THE SCRUBBING FRENZY IS ON HER AGAIN!
DIK BROWNE
WHEN SHE'S LIKE THIS *NOTHING* IS SAFE FROM HER!
NOW SHE'S WASHING THE DUCKS!

YOU SHOW NO RESPECT!
JUST WAIT TILL YOUR FATHER GETS HOME!

HEY! I **AM** HOME!
OH...SORRY, I DIDN'T NOTICE YOU THERE!
DIK BROWNE

WHY DO YOU CRACK YOUR KNUCKLES LIKE THAT ?!
CRACK!

DIK BROWNE
JUST BORED...
CRAK!

DOES HAGAR GIVE YOU A HAND AROUND THE HOUSE?
OH, SURE– I'LL SHOW YOU
HAGAR, CAN YOU HELP ME MAKE THE BED?
SEE?
DIK BROWNE

WHAT A WINDSTORM! IT BLEW THE ROOF RIGHT OFF OUR HOUSE!
CHEER UP... AT LEAST THE WORST IS OVER
DIK BROWNE

SIGH

IS THIS WHERE YOU GET TAX RETURNS?
YES, IN-DEEDIE!

WOULD YOU LIKE THE SHORT FORM OR THE LONG FORM?
DIK BROWNE

THE FRENCH ARE VERY TRICKY FIGHTERS
I HOPE THEY DON'T CATCH US IN THIS FOREST!
WE'RE ALMOST THROUGH!
KNOCK WOOD!
KNOCK KNOCK
OUI?
DIK BROWNE

OKAY! I APOLOGIZE!
REMEMBER OUR RULE!

WE NEVER GO TO BED MAD!
DIK BROWNE

AS YOU GO THROUGH LIFE THERE ARE THREE THINGS TO REMEMBER— "NEVER APOLOGIZE —NEVER EXPLAIN!"
DIK BROWNE
WHAT'S THE THIRD?
"DON'T GET CAUGHT"

IT'S BEEN RAINING FOR A WEEK AND THE MEN ARE IN A DANGEROUS MOOD, HAGAR!
NONSENSE!

DIK BROWNE
TELL THEM VIKINGS DON'T COMPLAIN!

I ONLY WANT MEN WHO ARE TOUGH!
MEN WHO CAN REALLY TAKE IT!
MARRIED MEN!
DIK BROWNE

STICK YOUR HEAD OUTSIDE AND SEE IF IT'S RAINING
RIGHT...
DIK BROWNE
CRASH!
...BUT FIRST OPEN THE WINDOW
RIGHT...
TINKLE!

SO YOU'RE CONFUCIUS! SAY SOMETHING WISE AND INSIGHTFUL!
OKAY
"FAME, LIKE A TIRED DOG, ONLY WAGS ONCE FOR THE KINDEST MASTER"
THAT WAS LOUSY!
THEY CAN'T ALL BE GEMS
DIK BROWNE

JUST RUNNING DOWN TO THE LOCAL STORE FOR SOME MORE HORRIBLY GOOD CARTOON BOOKS, COLOUR ALBUMS, CALENDARS, DIARIES, REMINDER CALENDARS, GREETING CARDS, GIFTWRAP AND TAGS – ALL FEATURING ME OF COURSE!
WHY NOT JOIN ME BEFORE THE BARBARIANS GET THERE!

Hagar Books to collect:

CARTOON BOOKS **PRICE £1.25**

Hagar Tries Again
Hagar Has A Go
Hagar In A Fix
Hagar On The Rampage
Hagar Gets It All
Hagar Leads The Way
Hagar Takes A Break
Hagar In The Rough

COLOUR ALBUMS **PRICE £2.25**

Hagar Lets Himself Go
Hagar In Trouble
Hagar The Hero

Prices and availability subject to change without notice.